Library of Congress Number 85-062344
ISBN 0-961-5623-0-7

Address all inquiries to:
Shannon Culver
The Monkfish Publishing Corp.
749 Airport Boulevard – Suite 1
Ann Arbor, MI 48104
(313) 663-3339

Budgie and Charlie,
Thanks for keeping me flying all these years.

Detroit.

Older than the Republic by three-quarters of a century. Car maker to the world. Proud of its history. Confident of its future.

A city of soaring towers and graceful roads. Of tree-lined streets and neat neighborhoods. Of tract homes in pleasant suburbs and high-rise apartments at the river's edge.

A city of industrial muscle and quiet parks. A place for churches and schools, for music festivals and football games.

But more than anything else, it is a city of people, most of whom came here from some other place, bringing little more than their willingness to be part of something important.

And they built a city that was not only tough and self-reliant, but one with its own unique style and beauty. A city whose vitality is as strong as its skyline and whose progress is measured every day in its offices and in its factories.

Dale Fisher's remarkable photographs have captured the special beauty of Detroit and the areas that surround it. It is a beauty that flashes in the gold of a summer sunrise, drifts toward the horizon on a wisp of smoke or ripples on the sunlit waters of a busy river.

Those who have taken this city as a part of themselves have never had reason to wonder why. It returns the affection in its own graceful way, in its own time.

It is a city that will always remember where it started – on the banks of a wide river one July day in 1701. But more importantly, it is a city that will not forget where it is going.

A city that understands that its heritage is its history and that history – though something to be cherished – is yesterday. Tomorrow will always be Detroit's challenge.

Michigan winter, Washtenaw County.

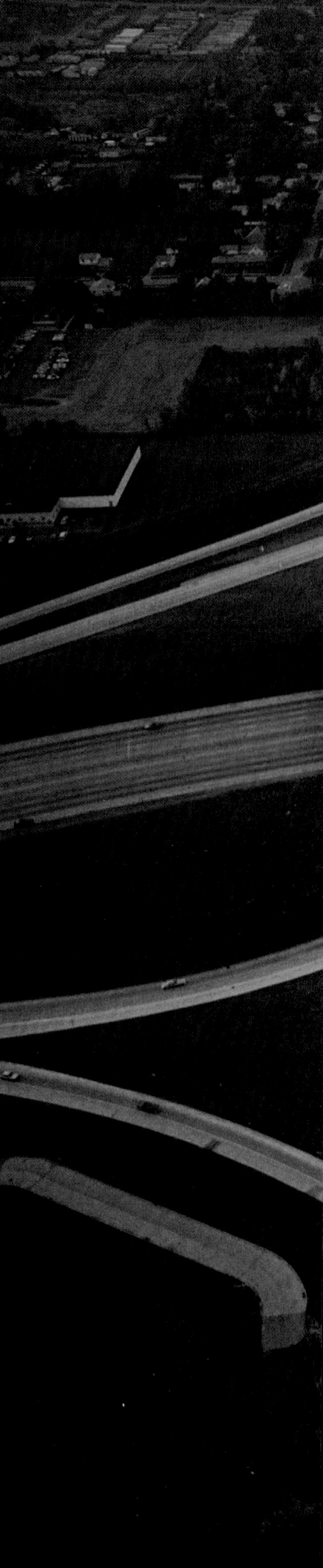

The interchange of Mound Road and the Walter P. Ruether Freeway.

The gilt cross of Saint Josaphat Catholic Church looking south toward downtown.

A holiday crowd on Belle Isle.

Grosse Pointe homes on the shore of Lake Saint Clair.

EDISON PLAZA

EDISON PLAZA

A city with baseball on its mind.

Belle Isle, a park since 1879.

Detroit begins its day.

Tiger Stadium on opening day.

WJR
INNING
AT BAT
OUT
STRIKE
BALL

STROH'S
OFFICIAL SOFT DRINK
STROH'S
STROH'S
STROH'S
Spirit of Detroit
Executone
U-22
RACING TEAM
U-1
Stroh's
MOBIL

Goodfellow Inc
RYDER

Car parts as art.

Stroh's Thunderfest, 1985.

An industrial seascape on the Detroit River.

Bus chassis as art.

Downriver's industrial muscle.

The Michigan Central Depot.

The General Motors Building and the tower of the Fisher Building in the New Center Area.

GENERAL MOTORS

GENERAL MOTORS

The Ambassador Bridge, Detroit's above water link with Canada since 1929.

River Place, headquarters of the Stroh Brewery.

Early morning in the New Center Area.

The Lansdowne, a fashionable floating restaurant.

AMBASSADOR
BRIDGE

TOWN
APARTMENTS

The
News

STROH'S
BEER

The
Free Press

TIGER STADIUM

GENERAL MOTORS

WONDER
BREAD

Their names in lights
– the signs of the city.
Bread, beer and bedrooms.
Engines, energy, editorials
and extra innings.

Headquarters of the Chrysler Corporation in Highland Park.

The morning sun brushes gold on the Renaissance Center.

Blessed Sacrament Cathedral and Chrysler Corporation headquarters.

Congregation Shaarey Zedek
Synagogue in Southfield.

Busy railyards.

Washtenaw County farm.

Southfield headquarters of American Motors Corporation.

American Center
American Center

15315

15532

Cargo containers as art.

The General Motors Detroit/Hamtramck
Assembly Plant.

The annual Port Huron to
Mackinac Race.

An island of faith in a city neighborhood.
Saint Florian Catholic Church
in Hamtramck.

Automobiles being loaded on rail cars for shipment.

The John C. Lodge Freeway.

General Motors Technical Center in Warren.

The excursion boat Saint Claire bound for fun at Boblo Island park.

STE. CLAIRE

The ketch Fancy Free.

Early morning commuter traffic.

The Windsor, Ontario shoreline.

The Belle Isle Bridge and the Detroit Boat Club.

Windsor looking to Detroit.

PARMALAT

Motor City's castoffs as art.

Windsor industrial waterfront.

Grand Prix auto racers on the streets of Detroit.

Uniroyal's "big tire".

UNIROYAL TIRES
ROYAL SEAL
UNIROYAL

AMBASSADOR
BRIDGE

Farming as art.

Saint Anne Catholic Church built in 1886.

Hamtramck is the heart of Detroit's sizable Polish community.

KOWALSKI SAUSAGE COMPANY WELCOMES YOU TO HAMTRAMCK-"WITAMY"
KOWALSKI

The Hiram Walker & Sons, Ltd.
distillery in Windsor, Ontario.

The skylines of Windsor and Detroit.

The Fairlane Town Center in Dearborn.

The twin Parklane Towers in Dearborn.

BROOKS LUMBER CO.

Suburban cityscape, Southfield.

Tiger Stadium, home of the 1984 world champions.

The gilt-topped dome of Saint John's Armenian Church in Southfield.

WWWW
106.7 FM
Budweiser
DOWNTOWN HOEDOWN
HART PLAZA
May 10,11,12
BASEBALL SOUVENIRS
CAPS • JACKETS • BUTTONS • CARDS • YEARBOOKS
PENNANTS • JERSEYS
ENTER ON MICHIGAN
Coke
Hennessy
the civilized way to keep warm
MIFFIES
Come up to Kool
KOOL
EMILY-MIDAS
DETROIT RUN!!!
15 1985
RYDER

CATCH A GREAT DEAL!
Ford
METRO DETROIT FORD DEALERS
SPORT SOUVENIRS
OPEN YEAR ROUND
M
GO BLUE
1444 SPORTSLAND U.S.A
CAPS • JERSEYS • BUTTONS
TEE SHIRTS • YEARBOOKS
JACKETS
SOUVENIRS
PARKING

FEDERAL LAKES
ST. CLAIR

Railyard as art.

Michigan Avenue and Trumbull is an intersection that means one thing to Detroiters...baseball.

Maritime traffic.

The Henry Ford Museum at world-famous Greenfield Village, Dearborn.

A railroad car ferry carrying boxcars across the Detroit River.

Motor City patterns as art.

A city of people, a city of homes.

The Horace E. Dodge and Sons Memorial Fountain in Hart Plaza.

BUICK
HYATT REGENCY

An ore boat unloading at the Ford Rouge complex in Dearborn.

The Hyatt Regency hotel in Dearborn.

The twin office towers of Phase II, Renaissance Center.

Flying high near Plymouth.

Ford Motor Company's automotive test track.

The afternoon sun touches the top of the David Broderick Tower in downtown Detroit.

Salem Spirit

Ford

Tugs and cargo containers on the Detroit River.

Ford Motor Company's world headquarters.

Grain silos at the Rickel Malt Company.

RICKEL
MALT
EST. 1876
RICKEL
MALT
EST. 1876

Spring in the woods near Ann Arbor.

The Veterans Administration Medical Center in Allen Park.

Old Saint Mary's Catholic Church in Greektown district.

MICHIGAN

MICHIGAN STADIUM
CAPACITY 101,701

The bird house at the Detroit Zoo.

Grosse Pointe Yacht Club on Lake Saint Clair.

Football Saturday in Ann Arbor.

The Book Tower in downtown Detroit.

HUDSON'S
HUDSON'S

CADILLAC
LELAND
EDISON

Renaissance Center landing pad.

The old County Building built in 1903.

N221CB

Washtenaw County deer.

Plymouth's annual Balloon Festival.

Meadow Brook Hall in Rochester.
Built in 1926.

The Detroit Tigers take the field at Tiger Stadium.

Cranbrook House on the grounds of Cranbrook Educational Community in Bloomfield Hills.

Softball City.

School buses as art.

The Detroit Medical Center.

The Memorial Tower on the main campus of the University of Detroit.

Getting ready for a concert at Chene Park.

A downriver winter industrial scene.

The Michigan State Fair.

First National Building's urban art.

Historic Fort Wayne.

The Michigan Blue Cross and Blue Shield Building.

A little bit of country in the city.
Eastern Farmers Market.

A November sunset.

The Westin Hotel in Renaissance Center.

THE WESTIN HOTEL

Republic

News

A working tug underway.

Detroit Metropolitan Airport.

A peaceful evening crossing.

With a roar and a roostertail,
powerboats race on the Detroit River.

929
7

Three seasons in Washtenaw County.

The Fisher Freeway.

Masonic Temple, a city landmark since 1922.

Hennessy
the civilized way.

EDIS

EDISON PLAZA
HUDSON'S
LELAND HOUSE
TOWN APARTMENTS

Madonna College in Livonia.

The Detroit Edison Company and the Edison Plaza office complex.

Hot slag at a downriver steel mill.

Runners on the city streets for the annual Emily-Midas Detroit Run.

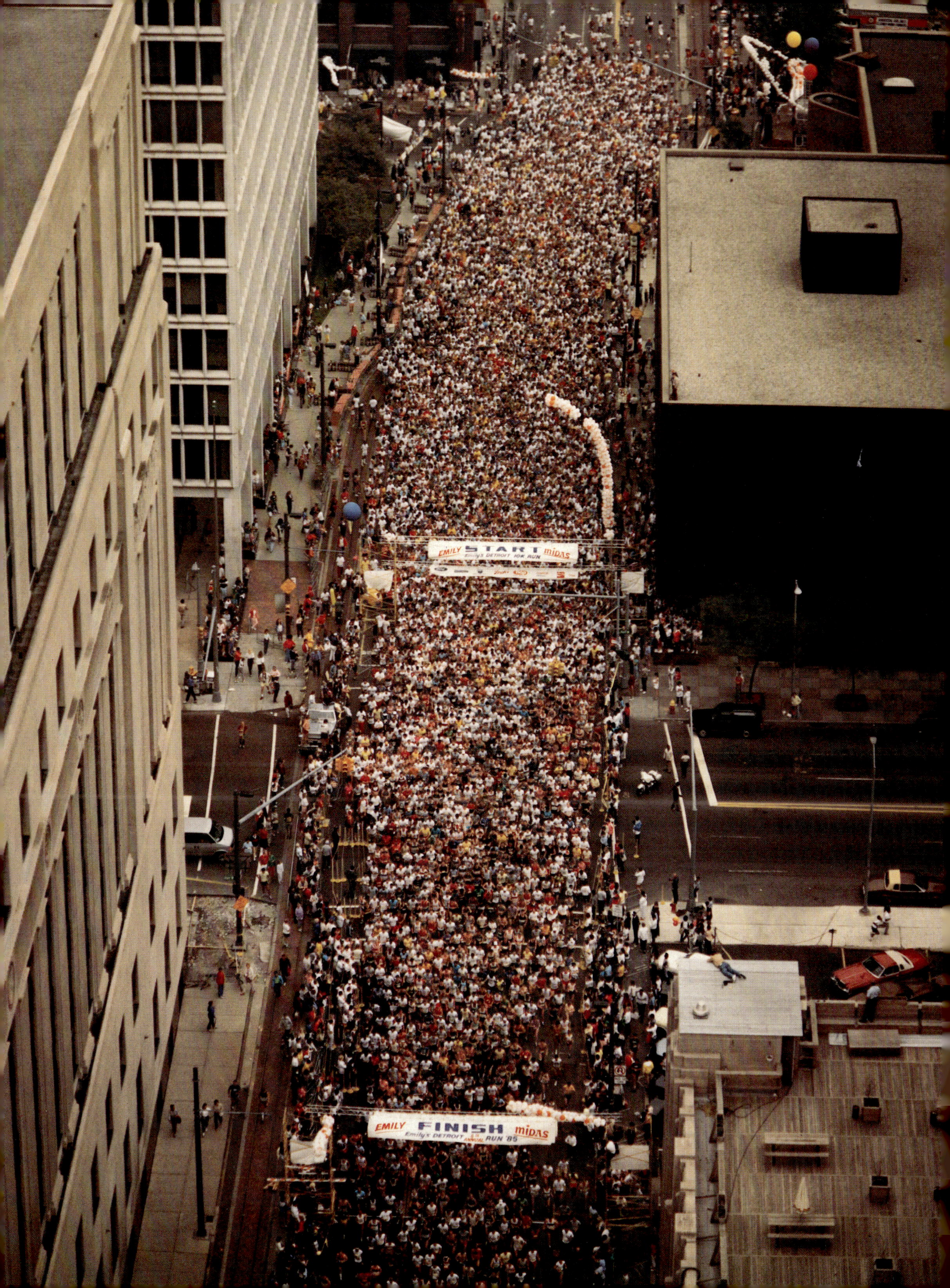
EMILY
START
Emily's DETROIT 10K RUN
midas
EMILY
FINISH
Emily's DETROIT ANNUAL RUN '85
midas

East
Lower Level
Lower Level

The main branch of the Detroit Public Library.

The Pontiac Silverdome.

In the city's Cultural Center, the Detroit Institute of Arts.

Automobile and Culture
Detroit Style
100 MASTERWORKS
American Association
of Museums
Annual Meeting

A new day in Troy.

Fishing for walleye in the upper end of the Detroit River.

Lafayette Park, a revitalized living area and Joe Muer's famous seafood restaurant.

JOE MUER
SEA FOOD

MOHAWK
GIN

Boxcars as art.

The twin skylines of New Center Area and Downtown Detroit.

Kirk in the Hills, a Presbyterian Church in Bloomfield Hills.

Boblo Island, the amusement park in the Detroit River.

Pleasure boats as art.

The international headquarters of K-Mart Corporation in Troy.

The city of Pontiac.

Through the late winter ice in the Saint Clair River.

INDEPENDENT
WILMINGTON DEL.

A project of this magnitude was accomplished through the devotion of a group of people who are very special to me, to them I give heartfelt thanks.

My associate of many years, Shannon Culver, who organized the book and much of my life during the past three years while the photographing was in progress, and Pat Monks who I regard as the "finest of helicopter pilots" who knows the areas we covered intimately.

For the early support and guidance of my close friends, Terry and Peggy Snowday, native Detroiters who love the city as I do and possess the desire to show its greatness to others.

To General Motors Corporation for their sponsorship of the initial printing run and their introduction to George Zuckerman, the "best of designers" associated with N.W. Ayer who provided invaluable help with the overall layout; and Neal Shine, the Senior Managing Editor of the Detroit Free Press for his editing and captions.

Detroiters Peter Stroh and Diane Edgecomb, and to Ward Fuller, President of American Steamship Company, all for their sage advice and continuing direction. To Nina Barwick, of Michigan Technical Institute, for her friendship, and loyality of many years.

Our photo printer Linda Winney, and Mike and Nancy Wolf at Precision Photo in Ann Arbor; to Village Press in

Traverse City, Michigan, and our liaison, Luana Dueweke, who presented us with the ultimate finished product.

I have seen Detroit as few others see it, from a helicopter. The colorful pattern of rooftops through the soft green of trees. The silver ribbons of freeways bending gently toward the horizon or turning in tight geometric patterns at an interchange. A river that is a wonder of nature, not just a commercial waterway and an international boundary.

I see Detroit's skyscrapers as monuments to its vitality, catching the first golden moments of a sunrise or dotting a darkened city with a million tiny lights.

My fondness for the area enhances my sensitivity as an artist. I was born in Ann Arbor and trained in aerial reconnaissance photography by the US Navy in 1952. In making this book I flew virtually every day with professional helicopter pilot Captain Pat Monks, and together we have captured Detroit in all its moods and seasons.

This collection of my art, photographed from the air, shows a city at work and at play. It reveals a beauty too often overlooked, even by people who share my affection for Detroit.

dale fisher